ZOOM
INTO SPACE

Helen and David Orme

ticktock

Copyright © ticktock Entertainment Ltd 2008

First published in Great Britain in 2008 by ticktock Media Ltd.,
Unit 2, Orchard Business Centre, North Farm Road,
Tunbridge Wells, Kent, TN2 3XF

ticktock project editor: Julia Adams
ticktock project designer: Emma Randall

We would like to thank: Sandra Voss, Tim Bones, James Powell and Joe Harris

ISBN 978 1 84696 698 9 pbk

Printed in China
A CIP catalogue record for this book is available from the British Library.

Picture credits
t=top, b=bottom, c=centre, l-left, r=right, bg=background
Julian Baum/ Science Photo Library: 45t, 73, 83b, 89t. Bill Brooks/ Alamy: 31cl, 31bl. Christian Darkin/ Science Photo Library:
14. ESA: 35b, 59, 79bl, 80, 81t. Mark Garlick/ Science Photo Library: 5tr, 46. Hubble Space Telescope: 49t, 50, 51. NASA:
1tl, 6-7 all, 8, 9bl, 12br, 15br, 17 all, 26, 27tr, 27br, 28, 32br, 33t, 33cl, 33b, 35t, 39t, 39b, 40bl, 41tl, 43b, 45br, 47, 48, 53t,
54bl, 55, 56, 57, 58, 60, 61, 62, 63, 64, 65, 66, 67, 68, 69, 70, 71, 72, 74, 76, 77, 78, 79tr, 82, 84, 86, 87, 88, 89bl, 90,
91, 92, 93. Reuters/ Corbis: 23b. Seth Shostak/ Science Photo Library: 75. Shutterstock: 11tr, 12bl, 19tl, 19cr, 24, 27tl, 34, 37t,
39c, 42, 54tr, 81b. ticktock Media Archive: OFC, 1br, 2, 3, 9tr, 10, 11b, 13 all, 15c, 16, 18, 19b x4, 20, 21, 22, 23t, 25 all,
29, 30, 31tr, 31br, 33cr, 37b, 38, 40c, 44, 49b, 85, collage rocket. Detlev Van Ravenswaay/ Science Photo Library: OFCtl, 4-5
original, 15cl, 36b, 52b, 53b, 83t.

Every effort has been made to trace the copyright holders, and we apologise in advance for any unintentional omissions.
We would be pleased to insert the appropriate acknowledgements in any subsequent edition of this publication.

Contents

Welcome to the Solar System

The **solar system** is made up of the Sun, the planets and moons, and many thousands of smaller objects such as **comets** and **asteroids**.

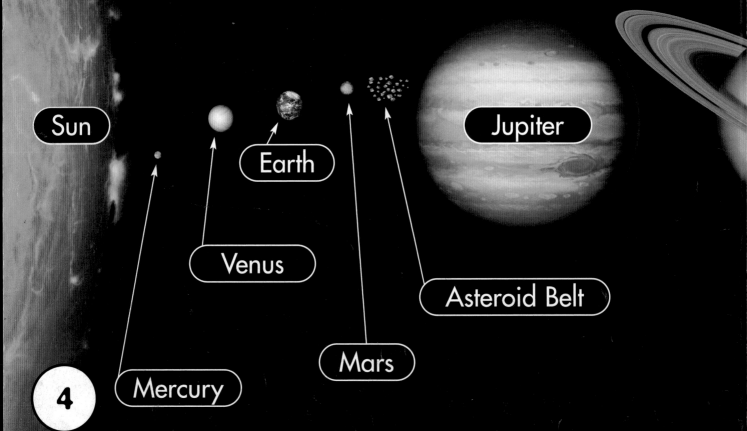

Sun

Earth

Venus

Jupiter

Asteroid Belt

Mars

Mercury

The solar system was formed millions of years ago from a spinning disc of gas and dust. Most of this material formed the Sun.

Spinning disc

Sun

Some material made the planets and moons.
The rest of the material made the comets and asteroids.

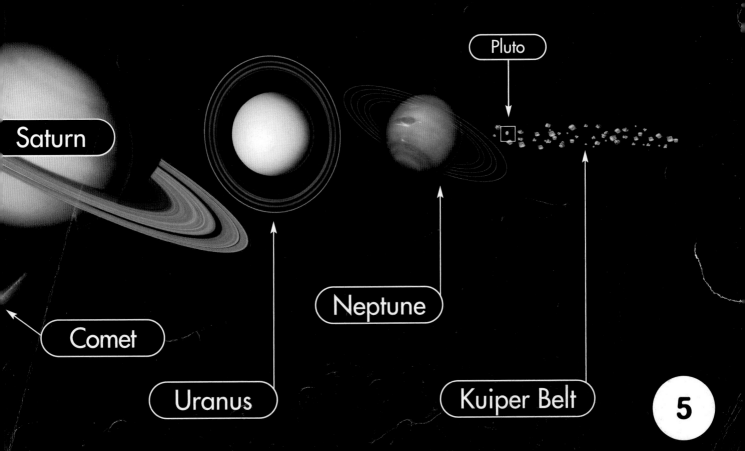

Pluto

Saturn

Comet

Uranus

Neptune

Kuiper Belt

Zoom to the Sun

The Sun is the most important object in the **solar system**. It gives all the planets heat and light. Without the Sun, life would not be possible on Earth.

Humans, animals and plants could not live without sunlight. Plants need sunlight to grow, and animals and humans need plants like vegetables and fruit to live.

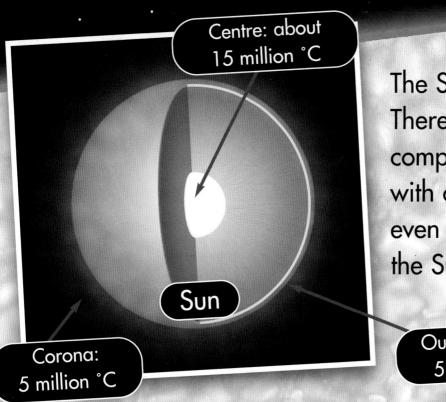

Centre: about 15 million °C

Sun

Corona: 5 million °C

Outer layer: 5,500 °C

The Sun is very, very hot. There is nothing we can compare the temperature with on Earth. We can't even imagine how hot the Sun is!

This picture shows how big the Sun is compared to the Earth. The Sun looks small from Earth because it is so far away.

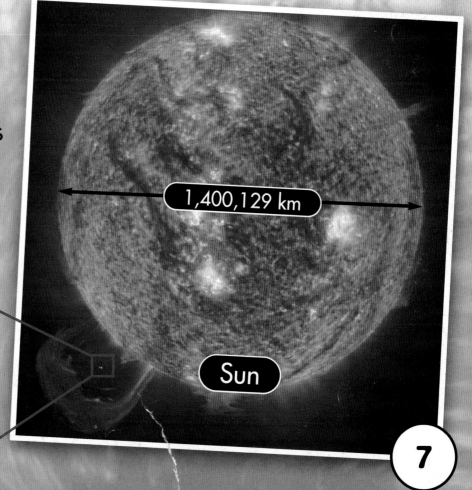

1,400,129 km

Sun

12,756 km

Earth

7

The Life of the Sun

The Sun is about four and a half billion years old! Like people, animals and planets, it was born, will have a lifetime, and then will die.

The Sun is made of **hydrogen gas**. The hydrogen gas is turning into **helium gas**. This creates a lot of heat.

Almost half of the hydrogen the Sun is made of has now turned into helium. It will take about five billion years for all of the hydrogen to be used up.

When all of the hydrogen has been turned into helium, the Sun will start to grow bigger. It will grow up to 100 times its original size! Then it will be called a Red Giant.

Sun

Red Giant

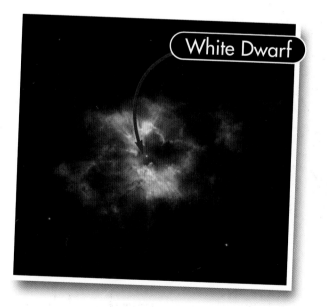

White Dwarf

Then the Sun's outer layers will start turning into a cloud of gas. The gas will slowly disappear and leave the Sun's centre. The Sun will start to cool down, although this will take millions of years. Stars like this are called White Dwarfs.

What is an Eclipse?

Sometimes our Moon moves between the Earth and the Sun. When this happens all or part of the Sun is covered over. This is called an eclipse.

Moon

This picture shows what happens when the Moon moves between the Sun and the Earth. The shadow marks the spot on Earth where you can see the Moon blocking out the Sun entirely. This is called a total eclipse.

This is a **partial** eclipse of the Sun. It means that only a part of the Sun is covered by the Moon.

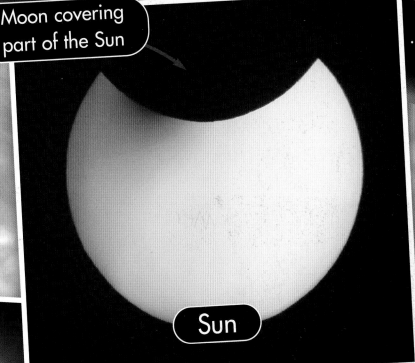

Moon covering part of the Sun

Sun

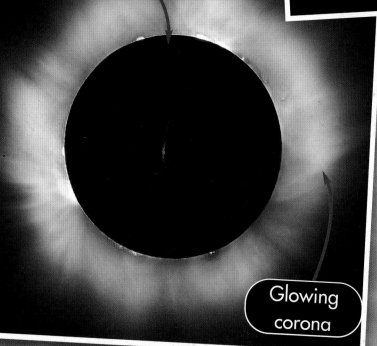

Moon covering the Sun

Glowing corona

This is a total eclipse of the Sun. It doesn't happen very often. When it happens, it is possible to see the glowing gas (corona) that is around the Sun.

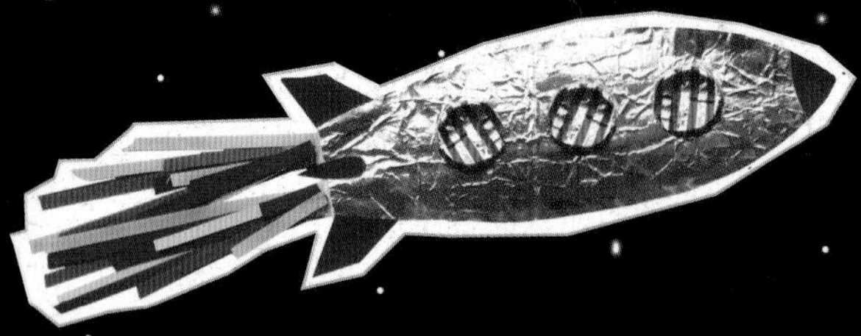

Zoom to Mercury

Mercury is a small, rocky planet. It is the smallest planet in our solar system. Mercury **orbits** the Sun faster than any other planet. It travels at 48 kilometres per second!

12,756 kilometres

Earth

4,880 kilometres

Mercury

Centre

Inside Mercury

Mercury is a very heavy planet. Scientists think this is because the centre of the planet is made of iron. This metal is very thick and heavy.

A planet is always spinning around.

The time it takes for a planet to spin around once is called a day. Mercury's day is the same length as 59 **Earth days!**

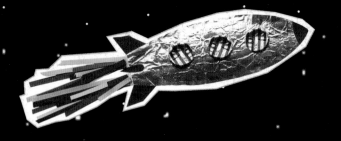

The surface of Mercury has huge cracks. They are hundreds of kilometres long and up to three kilometres high! The cracks were probably made millions of years ago.

3 kilometres

Mercury was very, very hot when it was a new planet. The huge cracks formed across the surface when Mercury cooled down.

Mercury also has one of the largest basins in the solar system. It measures about 1,350 km across!

The Caloris Basin was created by a huge rock hitting the surface of Mercury. Vibrations went right through Mercury and cracked the surface on the other side!

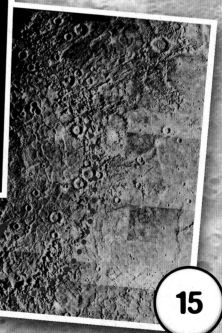

This is a photograph of half of the Caloris Basin.

15

Zoom to Venus

Venus is a very hot planet. It is covered in very thick clouds. We cannot see through these clouds with a telescope. But space probes have taken pictures of the surface.

This is a drawing of Venus' surface. It is mostly flat and very dry. There is no water on Venus.

12,756 kilometres

12,103 kilometres

Earth

Venus

Venus is almost the same size as Earth.
That's why it is sometimes called Earth's twin.

A day on Venus is 243 Earth days long.

The time it takes a planet to orbit the sun is called a year. A year on Venus lasts 225 Earth days.

Venus spins in the opposite direction of Earth.

17

Why is Venus so Hot?

The **atmosphere** on Venus is mostly made of a gas called **carbon dioxide.** This gas stops nearly all of the heat on Venus from escaping into space. People worry that Earth may become like Venus.

Sun

The heat from the Sun reaches Venus' surface.

The thick atmosphere stops it escaping, so the planet can never cool down.

Venus

Atmosphere

On Earth, we make a lot of carbon dioxide. We make it when we burn oil or coal. Cars, factories and planes all make this gas.

The gas gets trapped in the Earth's atmosphere. It stops heat escaping from Earth. We call this **global warming**.

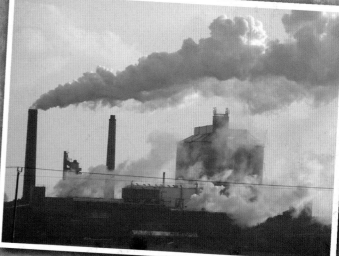

Could the Earth end up hot and dry like Venus?

Earth today ● ● ● ● ● ● ● ● ● ● ● ● Earth in future?

Zoom to Earth

The Earth is the only known planet in our solar system with **liquid** water on its surface. Over three quarters of our planet is covered by water.

A day on Earth is 24 hours long. A year on Earth is 365 days long, or 366 in leap years.

12,756 kilometres

Earth

The blue areas are water.

The brown areas are land.

The white areas are clouds.

Daytime

Nighttime

This artwork shows the Earth as it spins around. One half of the planet faces away from the Sun. It is in the dark. The other half is in the sunlight.

The Earth has two places called poles: the North Pole and the South Pole. These are at the top and bottom of the planet. The Sun does not shine very strongly at the Poles, so they are cold and icy all year round.

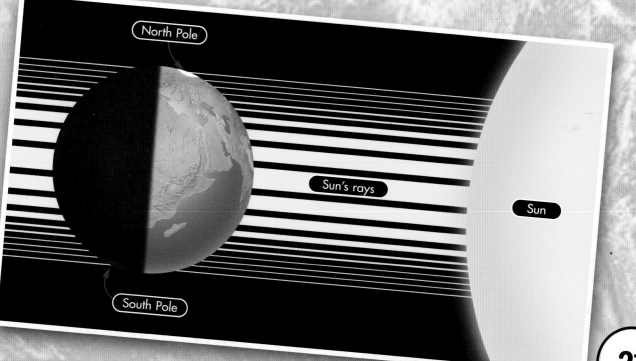

North Pole

Sun's rays

Sun

South Pole

Inside Our Planet

Planet Earth is a huge ball of rock. It is made of four layers. The centre of the Earth is called its core. The inside of the planet is very hot.

Earth has an inner and an outer core. They are mainly made of **iron**. The inner core is the hottest part of Earth.

This layer is the mantle. It is made of red-hot rock. Some of it is **molten rock**.

The crust of the Earth is the part that we live on. It is made up of land and oceans. It floats on top of the mantle.

Inside Earth

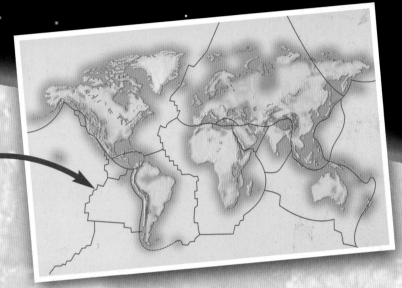

The Earth's crust is split into sections called **plates**. The plates are moving very slowly all the time.

The red lines on this map show the edges of the plates. They fit together like a jigsaw puzzle!

Sometimes, when the plates move, the Earth shakes so much that the ground shudders and cracks. We call this an earthquake.

23

Exploring Earth

We **still don't know**
everything there is to know about
Earth. But **satellites** and robots
help us find out more about our planet.

Sahara Desert

Satellites can take photographs of wide areas of land.
This helps us make very exact maps of large regions
of the Earth. It also allows us to see what the Earth
looks like from space.

Robots can be used to explore and take pictures of the deepest parts of the ocean.

Some robots look for **oil** and **minerals**.

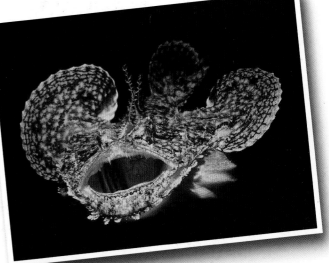

Some robots can study animals that live in the deepest oceans, such as this fish.

Zoom to the Moon

The Moon is much smaller than the Earth. It has no atmosphere and no life. The surface of the Moon hasn't changed for millions of years.

This is the surface of the Moon. It is rocky, dry and dusty.

12,756 kilometres

Earth

5,594 kilometres

Moon

The Moon is less than half the size of the Earth!

Like the Earth, the Moon is always spinning. One day on the Moon is about 27 Earth days long. The Moon travels round the Earth about every 27 Earth days.

Moon

27

The Moon's Changing Shape

When we look at the Moon from Earth over a few nights, it looks like it is changing shape. This is because we can only see the part of the Moon that the Sun is shining on.

Sometimes we can see all of the Moon. We call this a full Moon.

Sometimes we can only see half of the Moon.

Sometimes we cannot see the Moon at all because of its position in space. This is called a new Moon.

Moon in orbit

Full Moon

Earth

New Moon

Sunlight

As it moves around the Earth, different parts of the Moon's surface are lit up by the Sun. The blue line on each Moon picture marks the part we can see from Earth.

Full Moon

New Moon

These photographs show how the Moon seems to change into different shapes during one month.

The Moon is in orbit around the Earth. This is because a special force called **gravity** holds the Moon and the Earth together in space.

Moon's orbit around Earth

Gravity also affects what happens on Earth. It creates the **tides** in the Earth's seas and oceans.

As the Moon moves around the Earth, gravity pulls the water in oceans and seas slightly towards the Moon.

High tide

We call this high tide.

At the same time, the water levels drop in other places where the force does not reach.

Low tide

We call this a low tide.

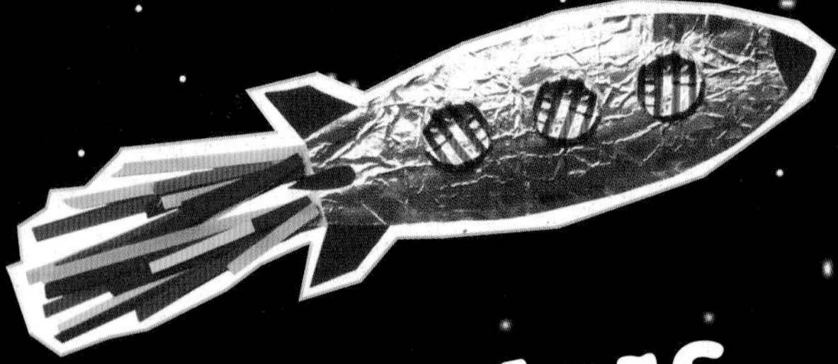

Zoom to Mars

The surface of Mars is dry with dusty soil. There is iron in the soil. The iron makes the soil red. Mars is sometimes called the 'Red Planet'.

Mars is almost half the size of Earth.

12,756 kilometres

6,786 kilometres

Earth

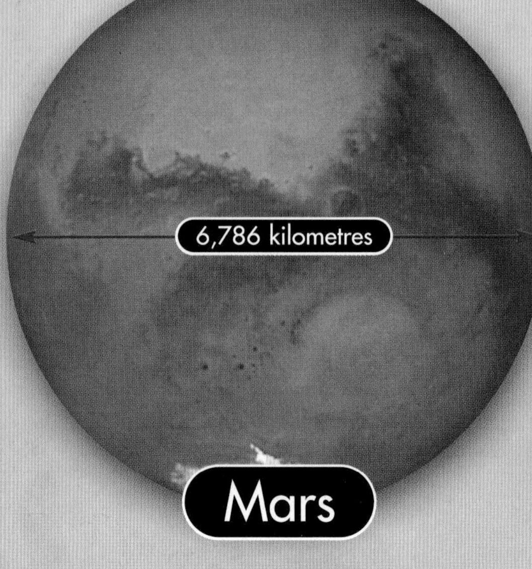

Mars

A day on Mars is just 41 minutes longer than an Earth day. However a year on Mars lasts 687 Earth days.

In the south, Mars has many mountains and extinct **volcanoes**.

In the north, the surface of Mars is flatter, with huge dusty plains.

Is There Life on Mars?

For hundreds of years, people thought that space creatures might live on Mars.

People wrote stories about Martians and other space creatures coming to Earth from Mars!

But life is only possible where there is liquid water. Scientists always look for signs of water when they study planets.

Some **astronomers** think these channels show there was once water on Mars. They believe these areas may be dried up rivers. If Mars had rivers, then it may also have been home to living things millions of years ago.

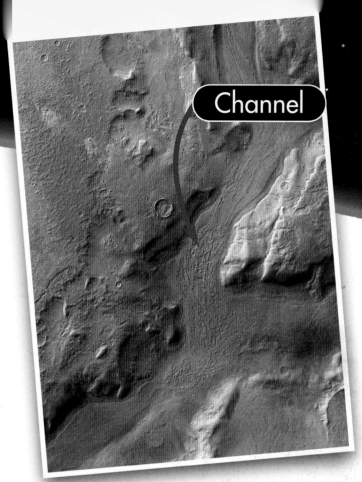

Channel

Frozen carbon dioxide on Mars

Space probes to Mars can only find frozen carbon dioxide. So Scientists believe that Mars is too cold for liquid water and life.

35

An asteroid is a rocky object, like a small planet. Most asteroids are less than two kilometres across, but some are much bigger. The first asteroids were discovered in the Asteroid Belt.

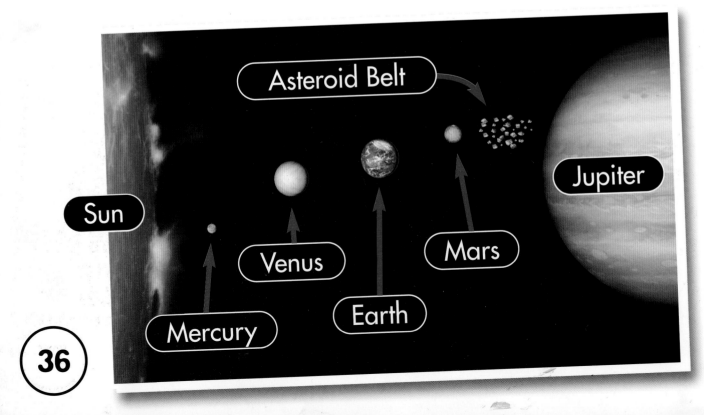

Asteroid Belt

Jupiter

Sun

Venus

Mars

Earth

Mercury

Shooting star

Some asteroids are not very far away from Earth. Very tiny ones often reach the Earth. They usually burn up in the atmosphere. We call these **shooting stars** or **meteors**.

Some meteors manage to reach the ground. They are then called **meteorites**. This is a picture of a meteorite that was found in Los Angeles in the USA in October 1999.

3.8 cms

Zoom to Jupiter

Jupiter is the biggest known planet in the solar system. It has a rocky centre, but the rest of the planet is made of hydrogen gas.

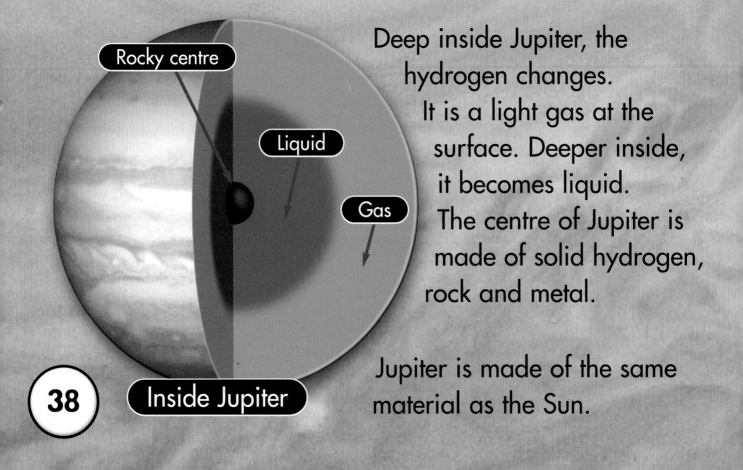

Rocky centre

Liquid

Gas

Inside Jupiter

Deep inside Jupiter, the hydrogen changes. It is a light gas at the surface. Deeper inside, it becomes liquid. The centre of Jupiter is made of solid hydrogen, rock and metal.

Jupiter is made of the same material as the Sun.

Jupiter

Jupiter is the biggest planet in the solar system. More than 1,300 Earths could fit inside Jupiter.

142,984 kilometres

12,756 km

Earth

Jupiter spins at 13 kilometres per second! It is the fastest spinning planet in the solar system. A day on Jupiter is the same length as 10 hours on Earth.

39

Jupiter has over 60 known moons! Our Earth only has one. Jupiter also has rings made of dust. The moons and the dust orbit Jupiter.

Jupiter's moons and rings of dust all orbit the planet in the same direction.

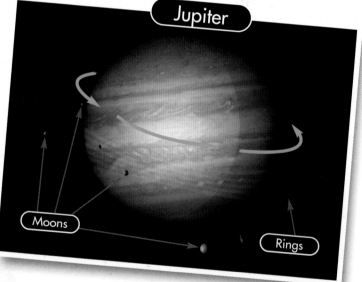

Jupiter

Moons

Rings

Meteorite

The dust was probably knocked off Jupiter's moons when they were hit by meteorites.

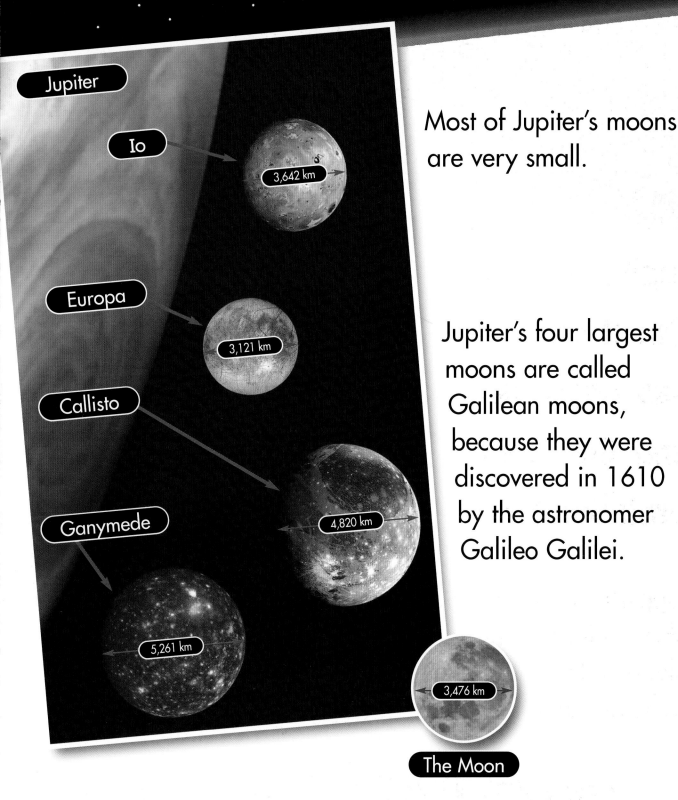

Jupiter

Io
3,642 km

Europa
3,121 km

Callisto

Ganymede
4,820 km

5,261 km

3,476 km

The Moon

Most of Jupiter's moons are very small.

Jupiter's four largest moons are called Galilean moons, because they were discovered in 1610 by the astronomer Galileo Galilei.

This picture shows how big Jupiter's moons are compared to the Earth's moon and Jupiter itself.

41

Zoom to Saturn

Saturn has the largest and brightest system of rings in the solar system. The rings are made of ice with some dust and rock.

Some chunks of dirty ice are as big as a house!

There are seven rings around Saturn. Some are very small and difficult to see.

Some rings are very thin. They are only about nine metres thick. That's about the height of a two-storey house!

The big rings are made up of many smaller ringlets.

The large dark stripes are the gaps between the rings.

Saturn's Amazing Moons

Saturn is the second-biggest planet in the Solar System. At least 56 moons orbit around it! Astronomers are still finding new ones today.

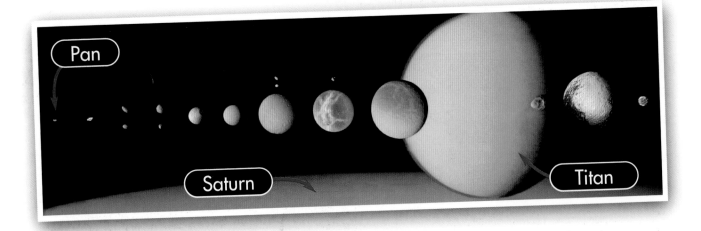

Saturn has moons of many sizes. Pan is the smallest moon that has been discovered. It is 256 times smaller than Titan. Titan is Saturn's largest moon.

Small moons near the edges of Saturn's rings are called shepherd moons.

Iapetus is a very strange moon because one half of the surface is coloured white. The other half of the surface is a dark reddish colour. The white half has lots of ice on the surface. Scientists don't know why the other half is dark, though.

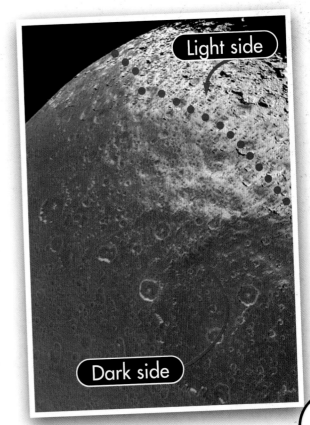

Light side

Dark side

45

Zoom to Uranus

Uranus is the third biggest planet in the Solar System. It has rings made of dust and rocks.

Astronomers found the first rings in 1977. The space probe Voyager 2 found more rings in 1986.

This picture of Uranus' rings is made up of many small photographs. They were joined together by a computer. The photos were taken by Voyager 2.

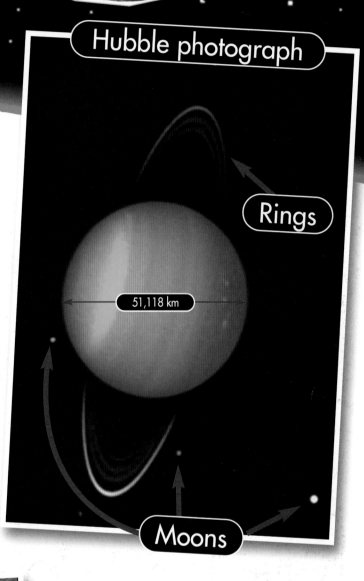

Hubble photograph

Rings

51,118 km

Moons

In December 2005, the **Hubble Space Telescope** discovered more rings.

Scientists think that when Uranus' moons are hit by rocks, dust and stones fly off into space and become part of the rings.

This painting shows how the rings would look close up.

The Moons of Uranus

Uranus has 27 moons that we know about. There may be more! The moons are named after characters in the plays by the famous English writer William Shakespeare.

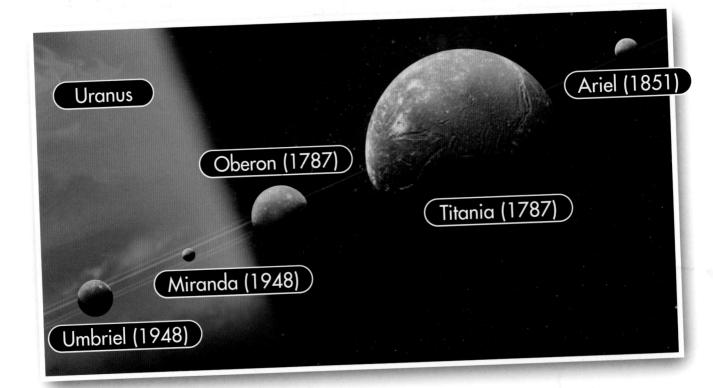

Uranus

Ariel (1851)

Oberon (1787)

Titania (1787)

Miranda (1948)

Umbriel (1948)

This painting shows Uranus's five biggest moons and when they were discovered. These moons were first seen through telescopes.

In 1986, the space probe Voyager 2 discovered another 10 moons.

Voyager 2

Atmosphere

This is Hubble above Earth's atmosphere.

The Hubble Space Telescope has discovered a further 12 small moons around Uranus! Some were not found until 2003.

Hubble can see Uranus's smallest moons even though they measure just 16 kilometres across and are more than four billion kilometres from Earth!

Zoom to Neptune

It is impossible to see Neptune without using a telescope, because it is so far from the Earth.

The best pictures of Neptune come from the Hubble Space Telescope. This telescope orbits the Earth out in space.

Hubble is 568 km above Earth's surface.

Because Hubble is outside of the Earth's atmosphere, its pictures are much clearer than pictures from even the biggest telescopes on Earth.

These pictures,
taken by Hubble, show springtime
on the southern half of Neptune. They show the bands
of clouds getting lighter in the south. This is a sign of
the Sun warming up this part of Neptune.

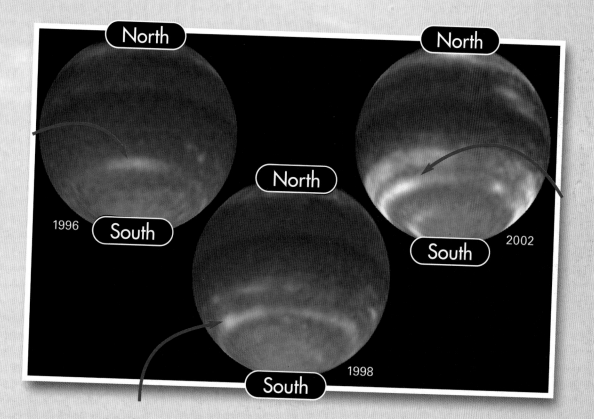

Because a year on Neptune lasts for
165 Earth years, springtime on Neptune lasts
for about 40 Earth years!

51

Zoom to Pluto

Pluto is a dwarf planet. It is only about 2,300 kilometres across. It was discovered in 1930 by astronomer Clyde Tombaugh.

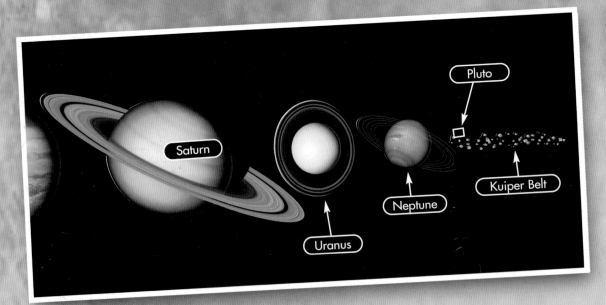

Pluto is part of the Kuiper Belt. The Kuiper Belt is a group of objects far out in the solar system, beyond the orbit of Neptune.

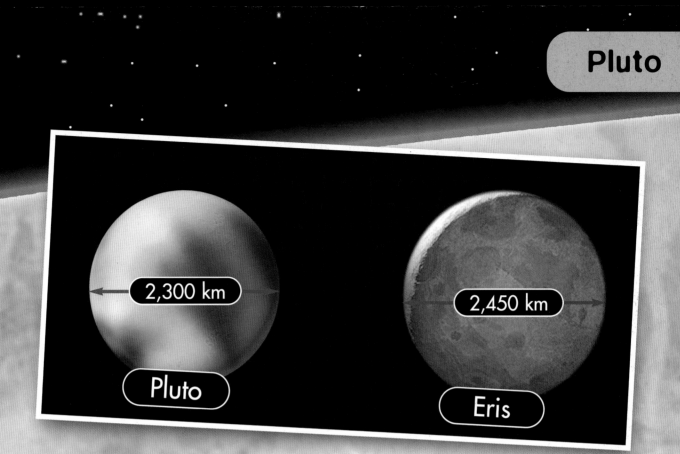

2,300 km

Pluto

2,450 km

Eris

The dwarf planet Eris was discovered in 2005. It is bigger than Pluto.

Kuiper Belt

No one knows how many more dwarf planets are waiting to be discovered.

Missions to the Sun

Scientists study the different rays coming from the Sun. This helps them understand how it affects the Earth.

Our atmosphere makes it very difficult to study the Sun. This is because it filters out many of the Sun's rays. The best way to study the Sun is to send space probes and **satellites** into space.

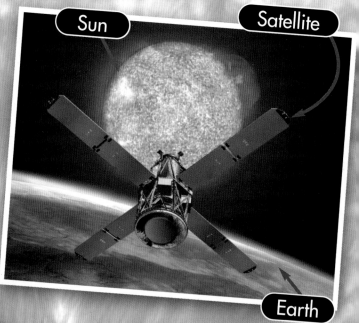

Sun

Satellite

Earth

Ulysses

This space probe is called Ulysses. It was launched in 1990, and reached the Sun in 1994. It has been sending back information about the Sun's outer layer and its rays ever since.

Sun

SOHO

This is the space probe SOHO (**So**lar and **H**eliospheric **O**bservatory). SOHO has been studying the Sun since 1995.

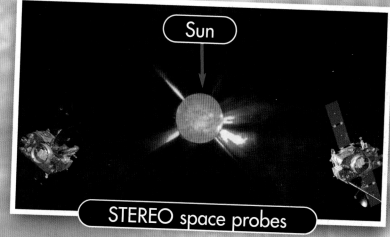

Sun

STEREO space probes

NASA is planning a new mission called STEREO (**S**olar **TE**rrestrial **RE**lations **O**bservatory). Two space probes will be sent to the Sun. They will take 3-D pictures of the Sun's flares.

Missions to Mercury

It is difficult to send a space probe to Mercury. This is because it is so close to the Sun. Unless scientists were very careful, the spacecraft would be burnt up by the Sun!

Sun

Mariner 10

Mariner 10 is the only space probe to have reached Mercury. It arrived there in 1974 and flew by the planet three times.

Mariner 10 managed three close fly-bys of the planet. It was able to photograph almost half of Mercury's surface. It also sent back information about the temperatures on Mercury.

45 km

Mariner 10 also took pictures showing more detail of the surface. This photo is of a huge **crater** on Mercury. It is called the Degas Crater. It is 45 kilometres wide!

57

Missions to Venus

There have been many space missions to Venus. Some space probes have even landed on the planet. The early Venus space probes were crushed by the atmosphere.

This is the Venera 9 **lander**. This Russian lander reached Venus in 1975. It was the first lander to take pictures from the surface of the planet. After sending the pictures to Earth for 50 minutes, it was destroyed by the heat on Venus!

The U.S. Magellan mission was launched in 1989. Magellan went into orbit round the planet to make a map of Venus.

This is the launch of Venus Express in 2005 by the European Space Agency. It arrived at Venus in April 2006 and started orbiting it. With its help, scientists are trying to find out more about the atmosphere of Venus.

Missions to the Moon

The Moon is the only place in space that people have visited. Six Apollo missions have successfully landed on the Moon.

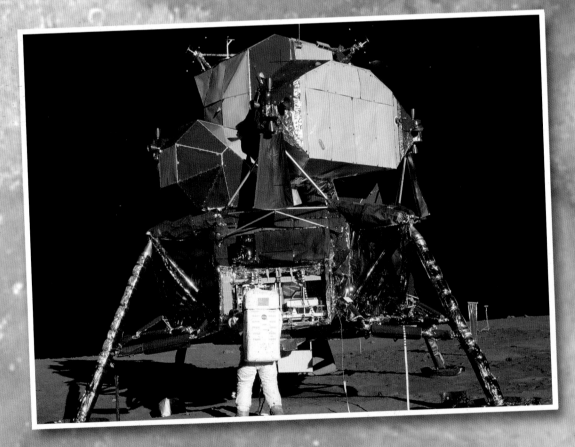

Apollo 11 was the first spacecraft to land on the Moon. This was on 20th July 1969.

The first man on the Moon was Neil Armstrong. He is on the left in this photograph.

As he jumped down to the surface, Neil Armstrong said, "It's one small step for man, one giant leap for mankind."

Buzz Aldrin was the second man to walk on the Moon.

When the Apollo 11 astronauts flew to the Moon, their spacecraft was in three parts.

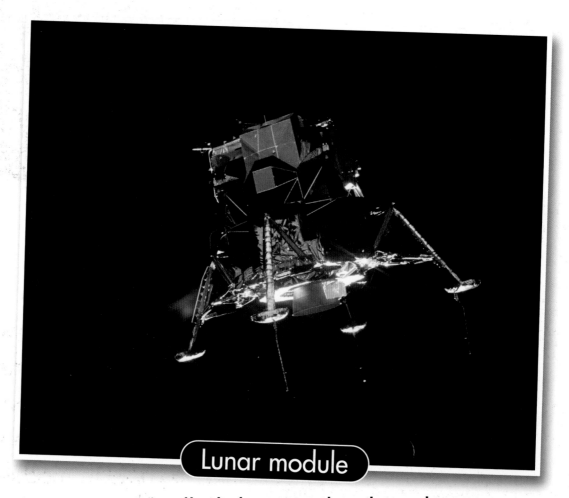

Lunar module

One part travelled down to land on the Moon, carrying the astronauts Neil Armstrong and Buzz Aldrin. This was the lunar module, called Eagle.

The other two parts, the command module and the service module, stayed in orbit around the Moon. The command module was called Columbia.

Command module

Earth

Moon

Eagle

When the mission was over, the lunar module took off using its own rockets. It joined on to the command module. Then the spacecraft carried the astronauts back to Earth.

63

Moon Buggies

The last mission to the Moon was Apollo 17 in 1972. The astronauts on Apollos 15, 16 and 17 travelled around the Moon using lunar rovers. A lunar rover is often called a 'Moon buggy'.

This is a photograph of the Lunar Rover on the surface of the Moon.

The Moon buggy was very light. It could travel across the Moon's surface carrying the astronauts and all the rocks they collected.

The top speed of the Lunar Rover was 13 km per hour.

Scientists would like to build a place on the Moon where people could live for many months.

Will there be a **moonbase** in your lifetime?

Missions to Mars

There have been many missions to Mars. The first successful one was in 1965. It was a space probe called Mariner 4.

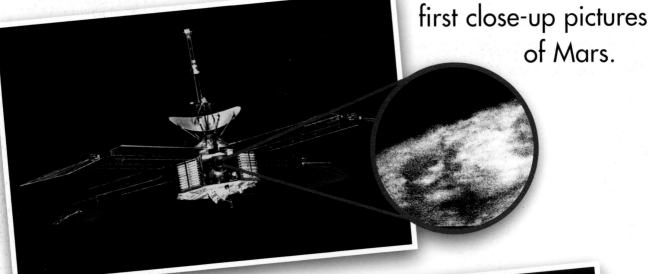

Mariner 4 took the first close-up pictures of Mars.

In July 1979, the Viking 1 lander became the first space probe to land on Mars. It took many pictures of Mars' surface.

Pathfinder rocket

Pathfinder robot

In 1997, the Mars Pathfinder rocket took a robot vehicle to Mars. The robot took pictures and tested rocks to help scientists learn about the surface of Mars.

In 2004, the Rover mission took two robots to Mars. These robots are still on the planet. They are looking for signs of liquid water on the surface.

Rover robot

67

Missions to Jupiter

No person has ever travelled to Jupiter, but many space probes have been to the planet.

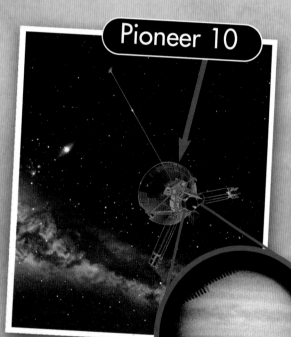

Pioneer 10

Jupiter

The first space mission to Jupiter was Pioneer 10. It flew past Jupiter in 1973. It took the first close-up photographs of the planet.

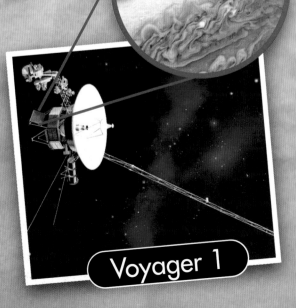

Jupiter's atmosphere

Voyager 1

Voyager 1 and Voyager 2 passed by Jupiter in 1979. They took photographs of the planet's atmosphere, its rings and its moons.

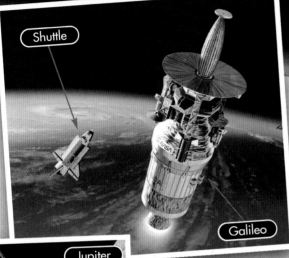

Shuttle

Galileo

Jupiter

Galileo in orbit

In 1989, the space probe Galileo was carried into space by a space shuttle. After the shuttle left Earth's atmosphere, it launched Galileo off into space towards Jupiter. Galileo flew through space and then went into orbit around Jupiter.

Volcano

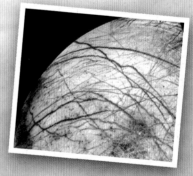

Galileo took pictures of the volcanoes on Io...

... and the icy surface of Europa.

Galileo also took this photo of a giant storm, the Great Red Spot.

69

Missions to Saturn

The most important mission to Saturn was Cassini-Huygens. The mission was made up of the **orbiter** Cassini and the space probe Huygens.

Rocket launching Cassini-Huygens

At the beginning, of the mission, Huygens was attached to Cassini. They were taken to space by a rocket. The rocket was launched in 1997. It reached Saturn in July 2004.

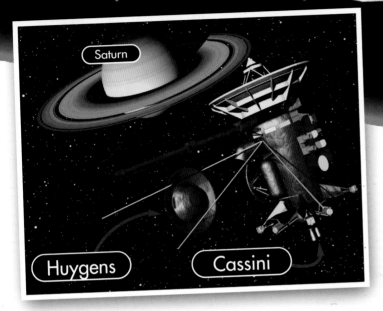

In December 2004, the Cassini-Huygens spacecraft separated into two space probes.

Cassini began orbiting Saturn to study the planet from space.

The Huygens space probe was sent to Titan. It travelled down through Titan's atmosphere to find out about the moon.

In this painting, we can imagine what someone standing on Titan might see.

71

Missions to Uranus

Voyager 2 is the only space mission there has been to Uranus. Voyager 2 discovered some of the planet's moons and that Uranus is tilted.

Titan-Centaur rocket

TITAN/CENTAUR COMPLEX 41

Voyager 2 was blasted into space aboard a Titan-Centaur rocket on 20th August, 1977.

The launch was at Cape Canaveral in Florida, USA.

Voyager 2 reached Jupiter in
1979, Saturn in 1981 and Uranus in 1986.

Jupiter

Uranus

Neptune

Saturn

A painting of Voyager 2's mission

After this it travelled on towards Neptune and the
edge of the solar system.

Missions to Neptune

There has only been
one space mission to Neptune.
The Voyager 2 space probe discovered
Neptune's rings and some of its moons.

Voyager 2 carried
powerful cameras and
many different kinds of
scientific equipment.

The Voyager 2 launch

Voyager 2

It travelled first to
Jupiter, Saturn, and
Uranus. It finally reached
Neptune in 1989.

Voyager 2 measured the temperature on Neptune and the speed of the wind on the planet.

Sun

Voyager 2

Neptune

Voyager 2 is now moving towards the edge of our solar system. Scientists hope it will send information back to Earth until 2030.

Missions to Comets

The first mission to a comet was in 1999. The space probe was called Stardust. It collected dust coming off a comet called Wild 2. It brought the dust back to Earth in 2006.

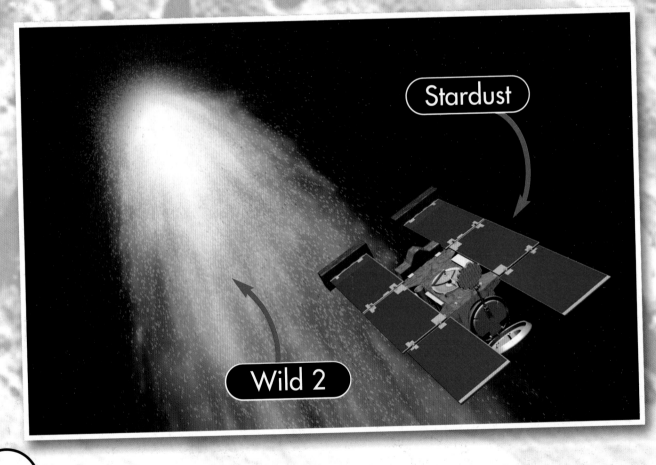

Stardust

Wild 2

Deep Impact

Tempel 1

In July 2005 the Deep Impact mission hit a comet called Tempel 1 and made a crater. This meant that scientists could study the layers below the surface of the comet.

Hayabusa

Itokawa

This is a picture of the space probe Hayabusa. It landed on the asteroid Itokawa in 2005 for one second. It collected samples that scientists will be able to study when it returns to Earth in 2010.

77

MESSENGER
(short for **ME**rcury **S**urface, **S**pace **EN**vironment, **GE**ochemistry and **R**anging mission) was launched by NASA in August 2004. It is the second mission to Mercury.

MESSENGER should fly past Mercury in 2008 and 2009. In 2011 it will go into **orbit** around the planet.

MESSENGER will photograph the surface of the whole planet. It will send back lots of information about the atmosphere and what Mercury is made of.

Painting of MESSENGER near Mercury

Painting of BepiColombo near Mercury

European and Japanese scientists have planned a mission to Mercury for 2013. It will be called BepiColombo. This should reach Mercury in 2019. It will help make a very exact map of Mercury.

79

Future Missions to Venus

Venus is too dangerous for people because it is so hot and has such a thick and heavy atmosphere. If we want to explore the surface in future, it will have to be done by robots.

The robots will be controlled by scientists on Earth.

In the future, scientists would like to send a mission to study more of Venus' atmosphere.

This is a painting of the space probe Venus Express orbiting Venus.

Usually, scientists look for **microbes**. Microbes are tiny forms of life. Some of them are found in the Earth's atmosphere.

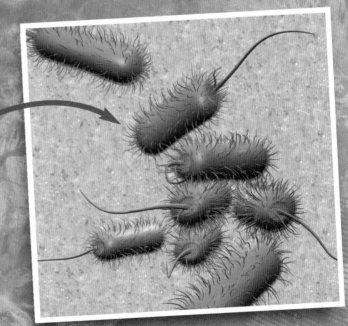

If microbes like the ones in Earth's atmosphere are found in the atmosphere of another planet, life there might be possible!

81

Future Missions to Mars

Astronauts have never been to the surface of Mars. But they may be able to in the future.

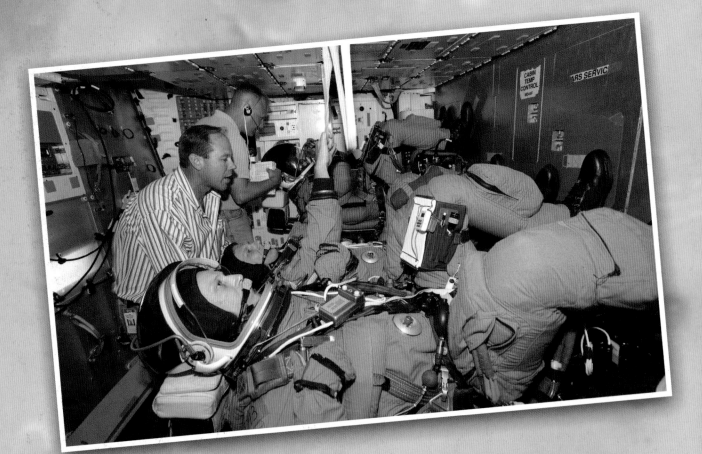

Astronauts will have to prepare very well for a journey to Mars. Flying to Mars will take nine months. It will be a tough mission.

Some scientists say it is possible to make a thicker atmosphere for Mars. It would take hundreds of years to do this. If it works, people could live in stations on Mars. They would have to wear space suits outside.

Then, scientists would have to change the air on Mars. This is so people could breathe the air and live without space suits. This could take 10,000 to 100,000 years.

If it works, people could move to Mars one day!

Future Missions to Jupiter

Scientists would like to send a space probe to land on Jupiter's moon Europa to look for life. This mission would be very difficult.

The probe would have to drill down through the ice on Europa to see what was underneath, as shown in this drawing.

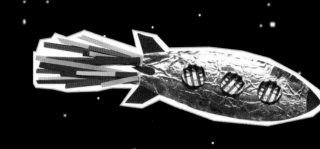

Earth has a place where scientists can practise the mission to Europa. That place is in Antarctica, near the South Pole.

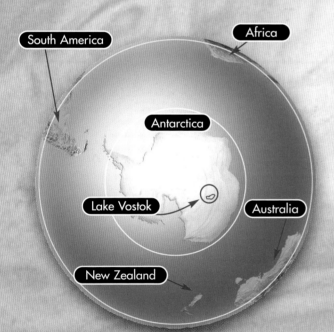

South America

Africa

Antarctica

Lake Vostok

Australia

New Zealand

Lake Vostok is a lake in the Antarctic that has been trapped under the ice for millions of years. The ice here is over three km thick!

Scientists are drilling through the ice at Lake Vostok to see what is in the water. Maybe one day they will try to do the same thing on Europa!

The scientists' camp

85

Future Missions to Saturn

Saturn's moon Titan has an atmosphere like Earth's was millions of years ago. Astronomers would like to find out more about Titan, because this will help us understand more about how the Earth developed.

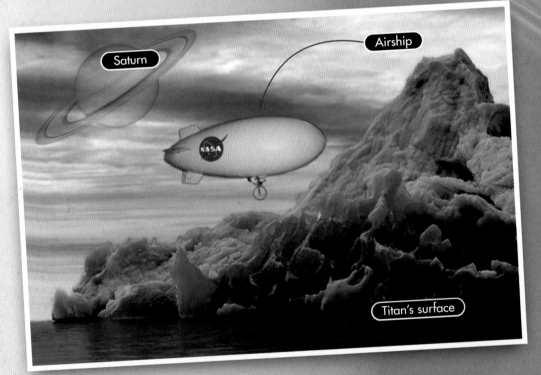

Saturn

Airship

NASA

Titan's surface

A future spacecraft might float in Titan's thick atmosphere. It could look like the craft pictured here.

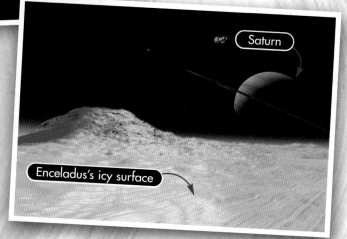

Enceladus

Scientists would like the Cassini space probe to do an extra mission and study the moon Enceladus in more detail.

Saturn

Enceladus's icy surface

The surface of Enceladus is covered in ice. There might be liquid water under the ice. Where there is liquid water, there might be life!

Future Missions to Uranus

Scientists are certain it is too cold for life on Uranus, but they would still like to find out more about the planet. At the moment, there are no new missions planned.

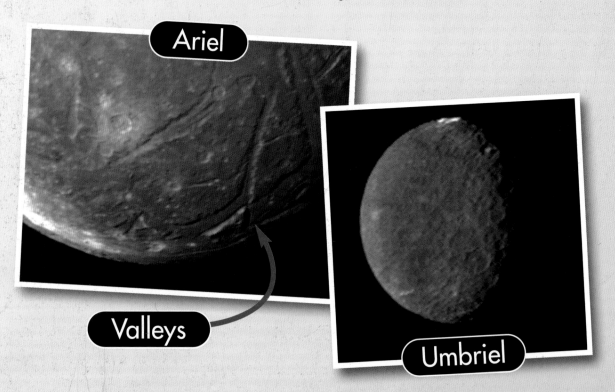

Ariel

Valleys

Umbriel

Scientists would like a closer look at Uranus's moons to find out why their surfaces are so different. There might even be more moons to find!

Any missions to Uranus will be done by robots. If astronauts went, it would take nearly nine years to get there, and nine years to come back again!

A painting of Uranus and its rings

Voyager 2 is carrying a special disc. It contains information and greetings from Earth. This is in case the space probe comes into contact with a faraway planet where there is life!

Future Missions to Neptune

NASA is planning a new mission to Neptune and its moons. If it goes ahead, the mission will be launched between 2016 and 2018. The spacecraft for this mission will arrive at Neptune in 2035!

Triton

The spacecraft will send two landers to Triton's surface.

In addition, space probes will be sent into Neptune's atmosphere.

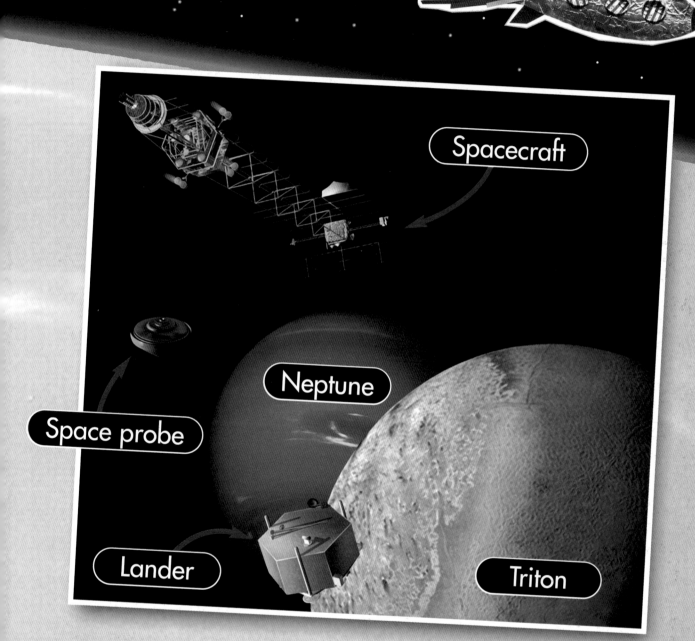

Neptune and Triton are very old. They haven't changed much since they were formed. Studying them might give us new information about how the solar system was formed.

91

Future Missions to Pluto

On 19th January 2006, the New Horizons space probe was launched. Its mission is to explore Pluto, Charon and the Kuiper Belt.

This is a photograph of the New Horizons rocket being launched.

The space probe will reach Jupiter by March 2007. It should reach Pluto in 2015. Between 2016 and 2020, it will study objects in the Kuiper Belt.

These are paintings of the New Horizons space probe above Pluto, and by the Kuiper Belt.

There is still a lot to learn about the solar system we live in.

Glossary

Asteroid A rocky object that orbits the Sun. Most asteroids orbit the Sun between Mars and Jupiter.

Astronauts People trained to travel or work in space.

Astronomers People who study space, often using telescopes.

Atmosphere The gases that surround a star, planet or moon.

Carbon dioxide A gas that is made when something burns.

Comets Objects usually made of ice and frozen gas that are in orbit around the Sun.

Craters Holes in the surface of a planet or a moon. They are made either by a volcano or when a rock from space crashes into the surface and leaves a deep dent.

Dwarf planet An object smaller than a planet that orbits around the Sun.

Earth days A day is the time it takes a planet to spin around once. A day on Earth is 24 hours long.

Earth year A year is the time it takes for a planet to orbit the Sun. An Earth year is 365 days long.

Global warming A process which heats up Earth's atmosphere. The burning of fuels like oil and coal gives off carbon dioxide, which traps too much of the Sun's heat in the Earth's atmosphere.

Gravity A force that pulls one object towards another. Large, heavy objects have more gravity than small, light objects. Because the Sun and planets are so large, they have strong gravity.

Helium gas A gas that is lighter than air. We use helium to fill balloons!

Hubble Space Telescope A telescope that orbits the Earth. Its pictures of space are very clear because it is outside of Earth's atmosphere.

Hydrogen gas A very light gas. The Sun is also made of hydrogen.

Iron A very hard and strong metal.

Landers Spacecraft designed to land on a planet or moon.

Liquid Something that flows easily.

Meteors Pieces of rock from space that burn up in Earth's atmosphere.

Meteorites The part of a meteor that reaches the ground.

Microbes Tiny living things such as a virus or bacterium.

Minerals Material from the Earth that is not a plant or an animal. Gold, silver, iron and salt are all minerals.

Molten rock Rock that has been melted and flows like a liquid.

Moonbase A place on the Moon that scientists may build one day. Humans would be able to live there for many months.

NASA (short for National Aeronautics and Space Administration) An American group of scientists and astronomers who research space.

Oil A greasy liquid that many machines need in order to work.

Orbit The path that a planet or other object takes around the Sun, or a satellite takes around a planet.

Partial When something is not complete.

Particles Tiny amounts or very small pieces of something.

Plates The separate pieces that make up the Earth's crust. They float very slowly over liquid rock.

Rays Beams of light and warmth. Some rays are dangerous because they are very harmful to life on Earth.

Satellites Moons or man-made objects that orbit around a planet.

Shooting stars Pieces of rock from space that burn up in Earth's atmosphere. Scientists also call them meteors.

Solar system The Sun and everything that is in orbit around it.

Space probe A spacecraft sent from Earth to explore the solar system. It can collect samples and take pictures.

Space shuttle An aircraft that can carry astronauts and machines into space.

Tides The change of the height of the surfaces of oceans. This change happens about every 12 hours.

Volcanoes Mountains where the hot, liquid inside of a planet bursts to the surface.

Index